*To those who have given us
the love and inspiration to write this book
Ed, Chip, Eric, Victoria, Bill, Lisi, Kaitlyn & Julia*

*Special Thanks for their contribution:
Mike Furman, Kellie Smith, Tristan Nutter*

RECIPES
for a
Beautiful Life

JULIE KEYE **and** MADALINE HALL

Recipes For A Beautiful Life

Welcome to a Happy and Healthy Life! We hope that after reading our book, your life will be enhanced with a stronger sense of wellbeing.

As important as it is to recharge our body through healthy food and exercise, it is just as important to recharge our minds through inspirational reading, prayer, meditation or just plain relaxing. Our minds and our bodies work together and we can control our daily outlook.

Each day, take the time to see or do one thing that has meaning for you, whether it is seeing beauty in a flower or a child, reading a poem or saying a prayer, making a special meal, taking a walk, doing something nice for someone or just doing something nice for yourself. If you find beauty in one thing each day, it will add up and result in a happier life.

Calling upon verses and Psalms from the Bible, these inspirational messages are framed by photographs of breathtaking beauty, from sun-drenched deserts to the glory of the white capped Rocky Mountains.

A charming addition to these messages is a sumptuous array of natural recipes for the enhancement of a woman's beauty and relaxation, using simple ingredients found in one's home. These long revered formulas for skin care, eye beauty, and body moisturizers, will help you to feel revived and pampered in a world that has too much stress and tension.

Take this journey now.
Let your emotions soar and go back in time,
when mothers passed beauty secrets down to their daughters.
You will welcome this opportunity to enter a special place.
Recipes for a Beautiful Life, awaits you
within the pages of this unique book.

Contents

PART ONE

Nature's Beauty and
Inspirational Bible Verses

"Be still, and know that I am God."
Psalm 46:10

In the beginning God created the heavens and the earth
Genesis 1:1

Create in me a pure heart, O God, and renew a steadfast spirit within me.
Psalm 51:10

And God said, Let there be light: and there was light.
Genesis 1:3

Two are better than one......If one falls down, his friend can help him up.
Ecclesiastes 4:9-10

Let my teaching fall like rain and my words descend like dew,
like showers on new grass, like abundant rain on tender plants.
Deuteronomy 32:2

And we know that God causes everything to work together for the good of those who love God and are called according to His purpose for them.
Romans 8:28

The desert and the parched land will be glad; the wilderness will rejoice and blossom.
Isaiah 35:1

I have not stopped giving thanks for you, remembering you in my prayers.
Ephesians 1:16

Ask, and it shall be given you; seek, and ye shall find; knock, and
it shall be opened unto you.
Matthew 7:7

Love thy neighbor as thyself.
Romans 13:9

I set my rainbow in the clouds, and it will be the sign of the covenant between me and the earth.
Genesis 9:13

Love is patient, love is kind. It does not envy, it does not boast.
It is not proud. It is not rude, it is not self-seeking,
it is not easily angered, it keeps no record of wrongs. Love does not
delight in evil but rejoices with the truth.
It always protects, always trusts, always hopes, always perseveres.
1 Corinthians 13:4-7

Gold there is, and rubies in abundance, but lips
that speak knowledge are a rare jewel.
Proverbs 20:15

"I have loved thee with an everlasting love."
Jeremiah 31:3

The fruit of righteousness will be peace; the effect of righteousness
will be quietness and confidence forever.
Isaiah 32:17

*But the fruit of the Spirit is love, joy, peace, patience, kindness, goodness, faithfulness,
gentleness and self control. Against such things there is no law.*
Galatians 5:22-23

The LORD is upright; he is my rock and there is no wickedness in him.
Psalm 92:15

You will be like a well-watered garden, like a spring whose waters never fail.
Isaiah 58:11

Let your light shine before men, that they may see your good deeds
and praise your Father in heaven.
Matthew 5:16

"Now faith is the substance of things hoped for, the evidence of things not seen."
Hebrews 11:1

Every good and perfect gift is from above.
James 1:17

We love because he first loved us.
1John 4:19

Consider the work of God; for who can make that straight, which
He hath made crooked?
Ecclesiastes 7:13

Feed the hungry, and help those in trouble. Then your light
will shine out from the darkness,
and the darkness around you will be as bright as noon.
Isaiah 58:10

Sing to the LORD a new song, for he has done marvelous things;
Psalm 98:1

Grandchildren are the crown of the aged, and the glory of children is their fathers.
Proverbs 17:6

I guide you in the way of wisdom and lead you along straight paths.
Proverbs 4:11

I am he that liveth, and was dead; and, behold, I am alive for evermore, Amen;
Revelation 1:18

Weeping may endure for a night, but joy cometh in the morning.
Psalm 30:5

Train up a child in the way he should go;
even when he is old he will not depart from it.
Proverbs 22:6

My people will live in peaceful dwelling places, in
secure homes, in undisturbed places of rest.
Isaiah 32:18

Sing to the LORD with thanksiving...make music to our God on the harp.
Psalm 147:7

God called the dry ground "land," and the gathered waters
He called the "seas."
And God saw that it was good.
Genesis 1:10

Delight yourself in the LORD, and He will give you the desires of your heart.
Psalm 37:4

*He leads me beside quiet waters. He restores my soul; He guides
me in paths of righteousness for His name's sake.*
Psalm 23:2-3

For whom the LORD loveth he correcteth; even as a father, the child in whom he delighteth.
Proverbs 3:12

The righteous will flourish like a palm tree, they will
grow like a cedar of Lebanon;
Psalm 92:12

Then the LORD came down in a pillar of cloud;
Numbers 12:5

Every man should eat and drink, and enjoy the
good of all his labour, it is the gift of God.
Ecclesiastes 3:13

*All the days planned for me were written in your
book before I was one day old.*
Psalm 139:16

For with you is the fountain of life; In your light we see light.
Psalm 36:9

You have put gladness in my heart.
Psalm 4:7

Let all that you do be done in love.
1 Corinthians 16:14

I came that you may have and enjoy life and
have it in abundance, until it overflows.
John 10:10

"..even the dogs eat the crumbs that fall from their masters' table."
Matthew 15:27

Better one handful with tranquility
than two handfuls with toil and chasing after the wind.
Ecclesiastes 4:6

*"And whoever welcomes a little child like this
in my name welcomes me."*
Matthew 18:5

*Who endowed the heart with wisdom
or gave understanding to the mind?
Job 38:36*

But they that wait upon the LORD shall renew their strength;
they shall mount up with wings as eagles; they shall run, and not be weary;
and they shall walk and not faint.
Isaiah 4:31

He covers the sky with clouds, he supplies the earth with rain,
and maketh the grass grow on the hills.
Psalm 147:8

Many waters cannot quench love, neither can the floods drown it.
Song of Solomon 8.7

"For I know the plans I have for you," says the LORD.
"They are plans for good and not for disaster, to give
you a future and a hope."
Jeremiah 29:11

If God is for us, who can ever be against us?
Romans 8:31

This is the day the LORD has made; Let us rejoice and be glad in it.
Psalm 118:24

"To everything there is a season, and a time to every purpose under the heaven..."
Ecclesiastes 3:1

Direct me in the path of Your commands, for there I find delight.
Psalm 119:35

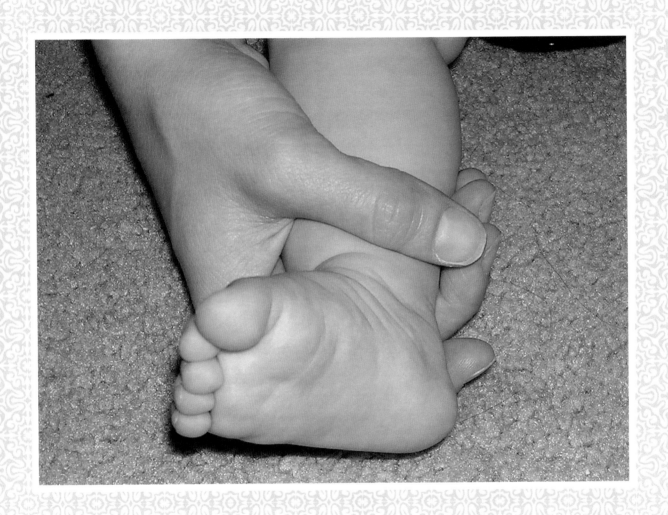

Thy word is a lamp unto my feet and a lamp unto my path.
Psalm 119:105

The pleasantness of one's friend springs from his earnest counsel.
Proverbs 27:9

*If the **LORD** delights in a man's way, he makes his steps firm;*
*though he stumble, he will not fall, for the **LORD** upholds him with his hand.*
Psalm 37:23-24

How many are your works O LORD! In wisdom you made them all; the earth is full of your creatures.
Psalm 104:24

Behold the LORD's hand is not shortened, that it cannot save; neither his ear heavy, that it cannot hear.
Isaiah 59:1

No one has ever seen God; but if we love one another, God lives
in us and his love is made complete in us.
1 John 4:12

Do unto others as you would have them do to you.

Luke 6:31

For the LORD is good; His mercy is everlasting, and
His truth endures to all generations.
Psalm 100:5

PART TWO

Relaxation and
Home Spa Treatments

"I'm having a Wonderful Spa Day at Home"

Bath Treatments

Herbs to use in Tub

❋ **Green Tea:** *Refreshing, antioxidant, helps with damage caused by sun*

❋ **Eucalyptus:** *Soothing to sore muscles, helps clear the mind and sinuses*

❋ **Peppermint:** *Cooling and relaxing aromatherapy*

❋ **Rose Hips:** *High in vitamin C, moisturizing, refreshing*

❋ **Ginger:** *Good for sore muscles, helps to open the pores and eliminate toxins*

❋ **Turmeric:** *Warming, antioxidant, good for muscles, cleanses the skin*

❋ **Chamomile:** *Relaxing, anti-inflammatory, antibacterial and cleansing*

❋ **Lavender:** *Relaxing, refreshing and cleansing. Ideal aroma-therapeutic solution*

❋ **Juniper:** *Drying, antibacterial, cleansing, purifying and effective aromatherapy*

❋ **Rosemary:** *Stimulates circulation, helps with fatigue, invigorating aroma.*

Mix 1 cup oil (olive, sesame or avocado), 1 cup mild shampoo, ¼ teaspoon of your favorite fragrance and pour mixture into running water.

Mix 1 or 2 cups of strong chamomile tea (or other teas) to running bath water.

Mix 1 quart of whole, cream or powered milk into running water to leave your skin soft and smooth.

Why is relaxation and pampering so important? We know that when we relax, we see the world around us differently. We take more time to stop and smell the roses. When we treat ourselves kindly, we are more likely to be open to those who may be in need of kindness and the opposite is also true; if you are kind to others you are more likely to be kind to yourself.

MOISTURIZERS

✳ *Lavender, aloe vera gel, shea butter and coconut oil are all good moisturizers. Aloe vera rinses off very well as a juice. You can add essential oils. Aloe is an anti-inflammatory and soothes irritated skin.*

✳ *Chamomile Tea bags are great for the eyes.*

✳ *Infused Calendula oil. Wonderful for sensitive skin. Can be mixed with aloe vera.*

DRY SKIN

✳ *Heavy cream or buttermilk mixed with a tiny amount of Rose hip seed oil or aloe vera: Effective gentle cleanser – removes makeup, impurities and excess skin oils without irritation. Leaves skin fresh and radiant.*

✳ *Vitamin E: Moisturizes and improves the skin's appearance*

✳ *Shea Butter: You can melt shea butter and add avocado oil, jojoba or olive oil*

✳ *Rose Water: A wonderful toner - Can be combined with essential oils - Add Chamomile for dry skin*

✳ *Almond oil: Contains vitamin E. Relieves itchiness, soreness, rashes, dryness, irritation and burns. Can be mixed with a little water to spread easily on the skin. Leave on for 5 minutes and your skin will glow.*

✳ *Wheat Germ oil: High in vitamin E. Good for moisturizing and soothing mature skin. Mixed with honey makes a great cleanser, which rejuvenates your complexion.*

When you help someone, you feel good about yourself. This holds true whether it is a friend, a member of your family, or even a stranger. Then, instead of being stressed about your problems, you endow yourself with an awareness of how many blessings you have in your life.

Oily/Troubled Skin

✳ **Cucumber:** *Soothing, cleansing and exfoliating*

✳ **Pineapple:** *Anti-inflammatory, high in vitamin C*

✳ **Carrots:** *High in vitamin A, calming*

✳ **Avocado:** *Moisturizing, high in vitamin E*

✳ **Hempseed:** *High in e.f.a's (essential fatty acids), moisturizes, gently softens*

✳ **Witch Hazel:** *Antibacterial, astringent, toning*

✳ **Aloe Vera:** *Soothing, moistening, healing, great for dry, sensitive or sun damaged skin*

✳ **Flaxseed:** *High in e.f.a's, increases circulation and leaves skin feeling soft and smooth*

✳ **Shea Butter:** *High in e.f.a's and anti-aging nutrients. Smoothes skin*

Essential oils for oily/troubled skin

✳ **Neroli:** *Calming, antibacterial*

✳ **Juniper:** *Drying, soothing, cleansing*

✳ **Ginger:** *Anti-inflammatory, soothing*

Each day, it is important to take some time for yourself. Whether you just sit back and listen to music, take a walk, exercise or take a bubble bath and escape from the world, you need to free your mind from everyday stress, rejuvenate and reflect.

OILY SKIN

TONERS AND EXFOLIANTS

Oily skin: *Witch Hazel with chamomile or lavender essential oils*

Problem skin: *Witch Hazel with juniper essential oils or ginger essential oils*

Crushed cranberries: *Good for cleansing. Add to blender with dandelion greens for minerals*

Essential oil of Tea Tree: *Put on blemishes. Anti-fungal and anti-microbial*

Essential oil of lavender added to toner or water, or aloe vera gel: *As moisturizer*

Crushed Walnuts: *Good exfoliant for dry skin*

Distilled water in a glass jar (not plastic) is best for essential oils. The scent will be longer lasting.

MASKS

* **Yogurt and cucumber:** *Good for inflamed skin, wrinkles and burns*
* **Raw honey and cream:** *Good for cleansing inflamed, dry skin, mature skin (warm over low heat)*
* **Fresh coconut water or grated coconut added to honey:** *Good for dry skin*
* **Pineapple:** *Not for sensitive skin. Good for troubled and mature skin*
* **Pineapple and cucumber:** *For mature, inflamed or puffy skin*
* **Carrots – grate and mix with avocado:** *For all skin types*
* **Honey:** *Kills germs on the skin and can reduce puffiness, giving skin a tight and youthful appearance*

Our treatments can soften lines and wrinkles, and do amazing things for your skin, but don't ever be afraid of growing older. My mother used to say, "Each age has its own beauty".

Normal to Oily skin

Banana Oatmeal Scrub

Mix ¼ banana mashed, 1 teaspoon heavy cream, 2 teaspoons of oatmeal and 1 teaspoon honey. Massage paste on your cleansed face and leave on for 15 minutes. Rinse with warm water then cold.

Carrot Mask

Mix ½ cup of grated carrot, 2 teaspoons mayonnaise and 1 teaspoon of heavy cream. Spread on cleansed skin and let dry for 15 minutes and rinse with warm water followed by cold. Carrots are high in vitamins A, C and potassium.

Normal, Dry or Sensitive Skin

Honey & Yogurt Mask

Mix 1 teaspoon honey, 1 teaspoon plain yogurt and 1 teaspoon heavy cream. Apply to cleansed face in upward motion, leave on face for 15 minutes and rinse with warm water and then cold. Honey is a wonderful anti-bacterial emollient containing enzymes, minerals, vitamins and amino acid, which makes your skin feel soft and smooth.

Refresh Mask

Mix 1 egg with 1 one teaspoon of honey and spread on face and leave on for 15 minutes. Wash off with warm water followed by cold.

Growing older means we improve; we have gained wisdom from life's experiences and our priorities are clearer. But we still need to take the time to keep ourselves looking and feeling our best.

<u>Rejuvenating Mask</u>

Mix 1 egg white with 1 tablespoon of cooked oatmeal. Spread on face and leave on for 15 minutes wash off with warm water followed by cold. Egg whites work as an instant face lift.

<u>Banana Bash</u>

Mash one banana with 2 tablespoon of honey and 1 teaspoon mayonnaise. Apply to face and keep on for 15 minutes. Rinse with lukewarm water then cold. Bananas contain vitamin C, B6 and potassium.

<u>White Whip</u>

Whip 1 egg white until thick and add ½ teaspoon of honey. Massage on face and leave on for 15 minutes. Rinse with lukewarm water and then cold water.

<u>Yogurt Scrub</u>

Mix ½ cup plain yogurt, 1 tablespoon raw honey, juice from 1 lemon and 1 tablespoon olive oil and massage on skin. Yogurt and honey are some of nature's best skin treatments. Honey brightens and smoothes and yogurt is deep cleaning and firms the skin.

<u>Cucumber Refresh</u>

Massage your face with slices of cucumber. Leave a slice of cucumber on each eye for 15 minutes for puffiness. Cucumbers reduce puffiness under eyes and reduce dark circles.

<u>Oil Facial</u>

Massage skin with Flaxseed oil or Olive oil. Remove with facial tissue. Great for dry or mature skin.

Spirituality, love, kindness, respect, appreciation, loyalty
and friendship intertwine with one another.
Treasure every moment and enjoy sharing time with those you care about.

Dry or Sensitive Skin

Cucumber Refresher

Mix one chopped slice of cucumber with 1 teaspoon lemon juice and add 1 egg white. Stir and apply to face and leave on for 15 minutes. Rinse off with warm water. This works as a natural astringent to tighten pores.

Chamomile Cucumber Eye Refresh

Mix soothing Chamomile tea with a grated cucumber and apply to gauze pads. Leave on eyes for 10 minutes for beautifully refreshed eyes.

Avocado Mash

Take one half of a large, ripe avocado and mash it together with 2 tablespoons of heavy cream. Massage it gently on your face and leave it on for 15 minutes. Rinse with warm water and pat dry.

Pore Tightening Mask

Mix one egg with ½ teaspoon apple cider vinegar and spread on face and neck. Leave on for 15 minutes. Rinse with warm water followed by cold. This will help tighten enlarged pores.

Oatmeal & Cream Mask

Mix ½ cup cooked oatmeal with 2 tablespoons heavy cream and 5 drops of essential oil of lavender. Apply to face leave on for 10 minutes. Rinse with warm water and follow with cold.

Have faith in God's love and you will never be alone.

Dry or Sensitive Skin

Apple Mask

Mix 1 grated apple with ½ avocado and 2 tablespoons heavy cream. Apply to cleansed face and leave on for 15 minutes. Rinse with warm water.

Strawberry Cleansing Wash

Mix 3 mashed, ripe strawberries with ½ cup plain yogurt and ½ teaspoon olive oil. Pat on skin, leave on for 10 minutes and rinse with warm water. This mask brightens and softens the skin and keeps it elastic and moisturized. It is also is a natural antibacterial.

Banana & Yogurt Mask

Mix 1 mashed, ripe banana with 1 tablespoon honey, ¼ teaspoon olive oil, 1 tablespoon plain yogurt and 1 egg white. Massage on face and neck and leave on for 15 minutes. Remove with warm wash cloth.

Yogurt & Carrot Mask

Mix ½ cup plain yogurt with 4 tablespoons honey, 4 tablespoons grated or steamed carrots. Apply to cleansed face and leave on for 15 minutes. Rinse with warm cloth.

Papaya & Mayo Refresh Mask

Mix 1 mashed papaya with 3 tablespoons mayonnaise and apply to face and leave on for 10 minutes then rinse.

Creamy Mask

Mix 1 tablespoon heavy cream, 1 tablespoon honey, 1 teaspoon aloe vera gel, and 2-3 drops essential oil of rose. Apply to face for 15 minutes and wash off with warm cloth.

Life's struggles enable us to become stronger. Each of us has the power to control our attitudes and use them toward a greater good.

Oily and Troubled Skin

Cucumber Mask

Mix ½ peeled, grated cucumber with 2 tablespoons aloe vera. Apply to cleansed face leave on for 15 minutes and rinse with warm water.

Tomato Cleanser

Cleanse your face and then gently wipe a slice of fresh tomato all over. Rinse off with warm water and mild cleanser followed with cold water.

Avocado Mask

Mix ½ peeled, mashed avocado with 1 tablespoon heavy cream. Apply to face, leave on for 15 minutes, and rinse with warm water and pat with Witch Hazel.

Ketchup Cleanse

Cleanse face and then pat on ketchup all over. Let dry for 15 minutes and remove with warm water and cleanser followed by cold water.

M of M Mask

Cleanse face thoroughly. Cover your face with a layer of milk of Magnesia and let dry.   You can wipe off after 10 minutes with warm water and rinse with cold.

Salt Facial Scrub

Add 1 teaspoon salt to 3 tablespoons aloe vera gel and mix together to make a paste. Very gently massage in an upward motion. Do not get too close to eyes. Remove with warm wash cloth followed by cold water.

<u>Each good day is a gift from God!</u>

A life open to God and filled with the beauty around you, sharing it with those you love, and finding time to relax so you can be the best you can be; these are the "Recipes for a Beautiful Life".

Oily and Troubled Skin

Flour Mask

Mix 1 tablespoon flour, 1 teaspoon vinegar, 1 teaspoon corn meal and 1 teaspoon heavy cream. Leave on face for 15 minutes and wash with mild cleanser and warm water followed by cold water.

Egg White Mask

Beat an egg white and apply to face. Leave on for 15 minutes and rinse off with cool water. Egg whites absorb oiliness and help exfoliate the facial skin.

Hair Treatments

Olive Oil Hair Treatment

A wonderful treatment for dry, scaly scalp: Apply ¼ to ½ cup olive oil to scalp, rub all over and leave on for 20 minutes. Rinse well and shampoo as usual. This can be done a few times a week.

Rosemary Oil Hair Conditioner

Mix essential oil of rosemary with ½ cup apple cider vinegar and apply to hair after shampooing then rinse off. Be careful not to get into eyes.

Pre-shampoo Conditioner

Mix 1 egg and ¼ cup olive oil and leave on hair for 15 minutes then shampoo and rinse as usual. Eggs are a great source of protein and will leave your hair nourished with a healthy shine.

Disclaimer

Please note that some people can have allergic reactions to natural ingredients and we recommend that you test any substance on a small area of skin (preferably on the inner arm area). If any skin irritation occurs, discontinue use immediately and remove all substance. If any serious complication occurs, please contact your physician. Please also note that you are using these recipe treatments at your own risk and we cannot be held liable for any reaction that you encounter while using any of these treatments. None of these formulations are meant to treat any serious medical condition. The information on these pages have not been evaluated by the FDA.

About the Authors

Madaline Hall was born and raised in New York City. She married and has two children. She entered the business community as an insurance broker working for a major company and was co-owner of Crafty Concepts, a craft business.

Her avocation for years has been her interest in all things literary. She currently lives on Long Island, New York and is dedicated to photography and writing inspirational works.

Julie Keye was born and grew up in New York City. She entered the film industry as an editor, working on many feature films. She married and has a daughter who served as a missionary in Japan.

In recent years, residing in California, she has written children's stories and film scripts, and most recently, collaborated with her childhood friend, Ms. Hall, on books with inspirational reach.

They met when they were eleven years of age and have been friends ever since. They feel truly blessed to enjoy a great friendship, and to have found God in their lives.

Made in the USA
Charleston, SC
08 May 2010

5162572R1